HARLEY-DAVIDSON

HARLEY-DAVIDSON

FACTORY AND CUSTOM DREAM MACHINES

Jim Lensveld

THUNDER BAY
P·R·E·S·S

1996 English language edition published by

Thunder Bay Press
5880 Oberlin Dr.
San Diego, CA 92121

ISBN 1-57145-030-0

© 1992 Rebo Productions, Lisse, Netherlands

This book has not been published under the responsibility of
Harley-Davidson, Inc.

Harley-Davidson is a registered trademark of
Harley-Davidson, Inc.

Printed in Spain

Library of Congress Cataloging-in-Publication Data

Lensveld, Jim, 1945-
    Harley-Davidson : An American Legend / Jim Lensveld
        p.   cm.
    ISBN 1-57145-030-0
    1. Harley-Davidson motorcycle--History.   I. Title
TL448.H3I46   1996
629.227'5--dc20   96- 13204
                                                CIP

Contents

A Harley-Davidson of 1915, with sidecar.

**A 1991 Springer Softail with a somewhat
nostalgic front fork.**

The Harley–Davidson Story

1903 stands out as a hallmark year in transportation history. Henry Ford introduced the Model A, and the Wright brothers succeeded in man's first airborne flight. An American institution was also born when 21 year old William S. Harley and his boyhood friend Arthur Davidson, both hobby designers, began seriously considering how to put their bicycle designs to practical use. A German draftsman who knew about early European motorcycles also worked at the same Milwaukee manufacturing company where Harley was a draftsman and Davidson a patternmaker. Using the German draftsman's special knowledge, in combination with Harley's earlier experience in bicycle building and the patternmaking skills of Davidson, they spent their spare hours experimenting in a basement workshop.

Although finances were modest and tools unsophisticated, the project progressed as far it could without the help of a skilled mechanic. Arthur Davidson's brother, Walter, happened to be such a mechanic, and because of a wedding, was soon due in Milwaukee. Bill Harley and Arthur Davidson wrote to Walter and offered to let him ride on their new motorcycle when he came. In the letter they forget to tell him that before he could get a ride on the motorcycle, he would have to help build it. On arrival Walter discovered the motorcycle in pieces, but the delayed, shaky ride was to change his life. As a machinist he could appreciate the close tolerances of the De Dion-type engine more than anyone else, and sharing the others' enthusiasm, he stayed in Milwaukee.

Shortly afterwards, William Davidson joined in the project, quitting a re-

The famous shed in the backyard where Harley and the Davidsons built their first bike in 1903.

sponsible job as a Milwaukee railroad toolmaker and foreman. As an experienced toolmaker he, with his brothers and Bill Harley, devoted every spare minute to putting the ideal in motion. Any mechanical problems they ran into were overcome with the assistance from the German draftsman, and a good friend lent the use of his shop, lathe and drill press to help complete the first Harley-Davidson motorcycle. Parts had to be fabricated from existing materials and American ingenuity. For instance, the first Harley-Davidson carburettor is said to be made from a tomato can. The first engine was a leather belt direct-drive affair capable of three horsepower, although when climbing hills it still needed leg power to back up the motor. Moreover a standard bicycle frame was found to be

too light for motorised travel. Harley's and Davidsons' goal to take the work out of bicycling was in need of some more time spent experimenting and at the drawing boards. On the next engine the fly-wheel was more than doubled in size, a satisfactory carburettor was designed by Ole Evinrude, and a loop frame was designed to replace the bicycle diamond frame. Now Bill Harley and the Davidson brothers were ready to put their idea into production. The calender had turned 1903.

The friend's shop had insufficient space for motorcycle production, so with the help of the Davidsons' cabinet making father, William, a 10 by 15 foot (3 × 5 m) factory was built in the Davidson backyard. A legend was born the moment they painted the name 'Harley-Davidson Motor Co.' on the door. As Bill Harley had engineered the first motorcycle, the Davidson brothers all agreed that his name took key billing. During 1903 the Harley-Davidson Motor Company built three single-cylinder, 25 cu. in (400cc) four stroke engines that produced three horsepower. All of them bought and paid for before completion. The first Harley-Davidsons took on the nickname 'Silent Grey Fellow' because the company took gray as their standard colour, and were of the opinion that motorcycling was to be kept a quiet activity. In 1913 their first motorcycle had known several owners and had covered 100,000 miles (160,000 km), while still fully functional on all its original bearings. Durability was the watchword from the beginning.

In 1904 the size of the original factory had doubled. Eight motorcycles rolled out of the door that year. A year later the building doubled in size again and in 1905 the first employee was hired by Harley-Davidson Motor Company. The first official main Milwaukee offices were erected in 1906 and production leapt to 50 motorcycles, with five extra workers to meet the demand. Bill Harley, and Arthur, Walter and William Davidson had by now given up their regular jobs and put all their time and energy into the company. In 1907 the company was established as a corporation. Walter Davidson became the first president, William Harley was chief engineer, Arthur Davidson became secretary and general sales manager and William Davidson was the works manager.

The single-cylinder had been enlarged to 35 cu. in (525cc) and now produced four horsepower. Production had been enlarged again also. Harley-Davidson now delivered 150 motorcycles a year and had introduced the revolutionary bottom-link front fork. The springer would be a standard feature on all models until 1949. Although the single-cyclinder Harley-Davidson of 1908 was popular with riders, with a top speed around 45 miles per hour (72 km/h), Bill Harley (who in the mean-

time had majored in engineering at the University of Wisconsin), continually searched for more power. Rather than change the successful design of the Silent Grey Fellow's single cylinder, Bill Harley decided to create more power through the use of twin cylinders: the 45-degree V-Twin. A design was born that was to become a Harley Davidson trademark.

While the motorcycle was essentially a utility vehicle, the growth of motorcycle sport was inevitable. Even during the earliest pioneer days, sporting motorcyclists tried competition events such as speed and reliability trials, endurance runs, and out-and-out racing. Up until 1908 the H-D Company ignored all types of competition, although numbers of H-D cycles were entered in all sorts of events by private enthusiasts. In June 1908 the Federation of American Motorists (FAM), announced the first large event of its kind to be held in the United States. It was billed as the 'Endurance Run' and planned as a two-day affair from New York to Brooklyn, to finish with a 180 mile (290 km) circuit in Long Island.

As the other factories were boasting of competition victories in the trade press, President Walter Davidson decided that H-D could no longer afford to ignore competition any longer. With an eye to the possible advertising value he decided to compete himself

on a standard model. More than sixty riders representing more than twenty makers of motorcycles started the Endurance Run on June 29th. By the end of the first day the rutted country roads had eliminated nearly half of the entrants whereas Walter was still in the running. The next morning he checked out with the other survivors for the circuit of Long Island to successfully complete the run. When the scores were tabulated, Walter was found to have made a perfect 1000 point record. Much was made of this victory in the trade press and established dealers reported increased interest and improved sales as a result.

Bill Harley, Arthur, Walter and William Davidson gave up their regular jobs and invested all their energy in building motorbikes.

In 1912 Bill Harley introduced the first commercially successful motorcycle clutch. Also new that same year were the centre post saddle suspension and the overhead intake/side exhaust valve combination that was used until 1929. A step starter was added in 1914 and three-speed sliding gear transmission and engine clutch in 1915. From 1916 the H-D Company began publishing 'The Enthusiast', the first genuine motorcycle magazine, to keep all H-D riders from all over the world informed on military motorcycle matters. During World War I, The Indian Motorcycle Company, H-D's main competitor, had been forced to sell its complete produc-

The first bike was powered by a strong, one cylinder 21 cu. in (350cc) engine.

tion to the army, so that commercially, Indian was out of the market. Harley-Davidson also sold part of their production to the army, but because of the good relations William Harley had with the Pentagon, H-D was never out of the commercial market. After the war, Indian lost its grip on the market completely, whereas Harley-Davidson became the biggest name in the motorcycle industry. Army green was replaced by the company's signature colour grey, but the army's demand for V-Twins had eventually led the company to drop the single cyclinder motorcycles in 1918. The twin was available as an F model (magneto) or J model (electric). One of Harley's few radical new model introductions was the new Sport Model that featured a new 37 cu. in (600cc) opposed fore-and-aft twin that produced six to eight horsepower and featured an enclosed chain final drive. The first model to carry a Harley-Davidson produced electrical system also appeared in 1919, a system which became the envy of the automobile industry of those days.

Refinements to Harley-Davidson motorcycles continued throughout the twenties. The company entered its third decade by introducing the first 74 cu. in (1200cc) V-Twin from which the legend would evolve. This new '74' was just the beginning of Harley refinements during the Roaring Twenties. Grease guns became the rule, with an alemite lubrication system with 12 fittings appearing on motorcycles in 1924. Drop forged, steel framed fittings came in 1925. The Teardrop gas tank made its inaugural appearance in 1926 on a new 21 cu. in (350cc) single, designated the BA model. Two years later the company was the first to install front brakes on a production motorcycle although at the time of their appearance, these met with some degree of rider scepticism. The WL 45 cu. in (750cc) side valve twin came along in 1929 and became an immediate hit, having the power characteristics of a Big Twin with the agility of a single. Here was a 16 horsepower machine that could reach a startling 70 mph (113 km/h).

Of course, 1929 also brought the start of the Great Depression. Motorcycle manufacturers went down also; dozens dropping from sight all together. A shortage of dollars for individual transportation, combined with low pricing and growth in the automobile industry, were at least partly to blame. Motorcycling had evolved into largely a recreational activity, and money for leisure activities was hard to come by during the 1930s. Harley-Davidson suffered along with everyone else, and sales fell sharply. However H-D prevailed where others went down. A strong dealer network, police and military use, conservative business management and a strong export business were all contributing factors. Sales may have slowed during the 30's, but the evolution of the motorcycle didn't. Two new engines were introduced in 1930. The 74 cu. in (1200cc) side-valve VL model and the new 30 cu. in (500cc) single arrived to keep the '21' company. The company also developed the three-wheeled Servi-Car in 1932, intended for use as a delivery vehicle.

In order to improve the sales, H-D decided to come out with special paint and styling treatments on their motorcycles. Gone was army green. Instead, Art Deco tank decals, two- and three-tone paint and other touches

for another unique Harley-Davidson twin, specially for desert use, which was called the XA. Only 1,000 left the factory doors before the end of the war. The 45-WLA therefore would carry the banner on its own during the War. In Europe every 45 cu. in (750cc) was known as a 'Liberator'. For each engine delivered, an enormous amount of spares were also built. Even now parts can still be had in the original wartime wrappings.

When the war was over, the first thing on every motorcyclist's mind was a new engine, to replace the one that had carried him through the early forties. During the first two years after the war there was no time for new models because of lack of materials, but unlimited civilian production resumed again in 1947. The first step Harley-Davidson took was to replace the 74 cu. in (1200 and 1300cc) and 80 side-valve twins with the hot new '74' overhead valve cycle that was initially taken into production in 1941. As a result of refinement during the war, H-D introduced a new 74 cu. in (1200cc) engine in 1948 that boasted hydraulic valve lifters and aluminium heads: the 'Pan-head' was born. Also given birth to was the Hydra Glide in 1949. A big twin with the first hydraulic front fork. It used helical springs, hydraulically dampened with oil. Two years later the Tele Glide telescopic fork would be introduced on the single-cylinder models.

During those hectic years in the forties, a new generation of Harleys and Davidsons were preparing themselves to succeed the company's founders. William A. Davidson had died in 1937 and H-D's long time President Walter Davidson passed away in his sixty-sixth year on February 7th 1942. Bill Harley died in 1943. Their passings were a heavy blow to the company they founded, but the family tradition continued. The last of the four founders, Arthur Davidson, died in a car accident on December 30, 1950, and from that time on the new generation of Harleys and Davidsons were on their own.

Major changes came in 1952 and 1953 when chrome plated piston rings were placed in every model. The 1952 K-model 45 cu. in (750cc) twin replaced the WL 45. It came with a low swung frame with hydraulically dampened

were added. The Harley-Davidson special styling expertise was born. As the sales of single-cylinder motorcycles kept on dropping, in 1934 they were taken out of production all together. The most important advances in that period took place in 1936. Because American riders were demanding more power, the company introduced the 80 cu. in (1300cc) side-valve twin and after that the overhead-valve twin. Because of the shape of the valves the new '61' became known as the 'Knucklehead'. It delivered twice the horsepower of the old '61' model and featured a double-loop frame, heavier forks and wheels, a four speed trans-

In 1909 the one-cylinder was honed to 30 cu. in (500cc), and it supplied four horsepower.

mission and the first oil circulation system.

In the fall of 1939, both Indian and Harley Davidson motorcycle factories received contracts to supply military machines to the Allied Forces. H-D's answer to this order was a heavy duty version of the 45 cu. in (750cc) 'DLD' model, which was now designated as the 'WLA' ('A' for Army). Production of military WLA 45s ran up to 90,000. World War Two was also responsible

front forks and rear suspension. When one of H-D's oldest competitors, Indian, passed from the American motor industry scene in 1954, Harley-Davidson was the lone survivor in a once overpopulated American motorcycle marketplace. In the spring of that same year, the so-called 'outlaw' element in motorcycling found its identity in a motion picture entitled 'The Wild One', featuring Marlon Brando. In 1957 the Original American Muscle Bike, the XL Sportster, hit the motor scene with a 55 cu. in (900cc) overhead valve engine. In 1958 the Duo Glide emerged from the Hydra Glide.

Because of increased imports in the sixties, Harley-Davidson had lost about 90% of its market. From 1960 until 1978 Harley imported Italian motorcycles to meet the demand for lightweight cycles. Target groups for the

The first official Milwaukee head office was opened in 1906.

company were police forces, paramilitary organisations and the so-called outlaws. But the outlaws were not satisfied with the way their Harleys left the factory, and many started to take off all extra weight. This is known as 'chopping' the American way. The movie Easy Rider from 1969 showed two of those Harley-choppers touring through the USA. Because of the movie's popularity, motorcycles regained some ground and many H-D riders started to chop their bikes. In Europe this took a little longer than in the States, but as from early 1970 choppers were seen on the roads more and more. Towards the end of the stormy sixties, Harley-Davidson passed into a new era. The company that was privately owned for more than

sixty years, went public in 1965 and merged in 1969 with the American Machine and Foundry Company (AMF).

The merger with AMF provided Harley-Davidson with the necessary resources for continued growth. In 1972 the all-alloy engine XR-750 totally dominated the racing world. Apart from racing success, Harley performed well in the heavyweight custom and touring markets. In 1971 the new FX Super Glide combined the power of the big V-Twin, with the front end of the Sportster. The Harley-Davidson line of 1976 consisted of an Electra Glide, two Super Glides, two Sportsters, six lightweights, and bicentennial 'Liberty' editions of the five existing V-Twins. The FXS Low Rider was introduced in 1977 and would inspire many models to come. The late seven-

ties brought the challenge of meeting increasingly stringent government environmental regulations. These laws resulted in changes to carburation, ignition and exhaust systems, and the company met all this with remarkable adaptability. However, during the annual motorcycle show at Daytona during Bike Week in 1981, the air was filled with big news concerning the company's future.

The AMF had done much to modernise the company and helped the Motor Company through a critical stage of growth. Now it was time for H-D to stand on its own two feet once again. The big news came on February 26, 1981 when a letter of intent was signed by a group of senior Harley-Davidson executives to purchase the Harley-Davidson Motor Company from AMF. During a press conference at Daytona Beach a week later, the positive aspects of the merger were revealed: AMF's substantial capital investments from 1969 through 1980 in the motorcycle and golf car business had permitted Harley-Davidson revenues to grow from $49 million to approximately $300 million. Now it was time for the company to look to the future with pride and expectation. The Eagle would soar alone . . .

Arnold Schwarzenegger on an Easy Rider, one of the Harley choppers.

The universally famous Harley–Davidson logo.

Golden Oldie
The '03–'04 Harley–Davidson Single

Antique bikes are getting as collectible as Ming vases and Elvis' scarves. They bring big bucks and promise to gain in value with every passing year. Harleys share that same distinction when people think of investing in metal as a good way to plan for the future. Few H-D's could be as historically valuable as this '03–'04 model, one of a tiny number in existence. Harley-Davidson were still in their infant years and hoping to make their mark as a commercial success when they 'updated' the first 1903 models, calling the new versions 1904 models for the new sales year. As a result this machine has taken on the name the '03–'04 model.

To keep the technological level of the time in perspective, it's important to remember that the Harley-Davidson Motor Company was born in 1903, the same year the Wright Brothers climbed a sand dune in Kitty Hawk, North Carolina and launched a spindly wood and paper aeroplane into history. William, Walter and Arthur Davidson, three brothers sharing mechanical skills, had recently teamed up with an engineer of some genius, William Harley, and launched their own piece of history, albeit two-wheeled and not two-winged. But the Harley-Davidson motorcycle would fly at least as far as the aeroplane in the imagination of the motorcycling public.

It's easy to think of this early Harley as a simple bicycle with an engine stuck between the wheels. The engine itself was a De Dion-type single cylinder, 25 cu. in (400cc) fourstroke powerplant that produced a whopping big 3bhp. All across America, other novice motorcycle builders were hammering away at their own two-wheeled won-

The mechanical heart of the first Harley was a De Dion one cylinder, 25 cu. in (400cc) power source which supplied 3bhp.

ders. The Davidsons and Bill Harley, working nights and weekends and keeping their regular jobs just in case, built, and very importantly sold, three bikes in 1903, two more in 1904 and eight in 1905. Things really started rolling when in 1906, 50 H-D's were built and sold.

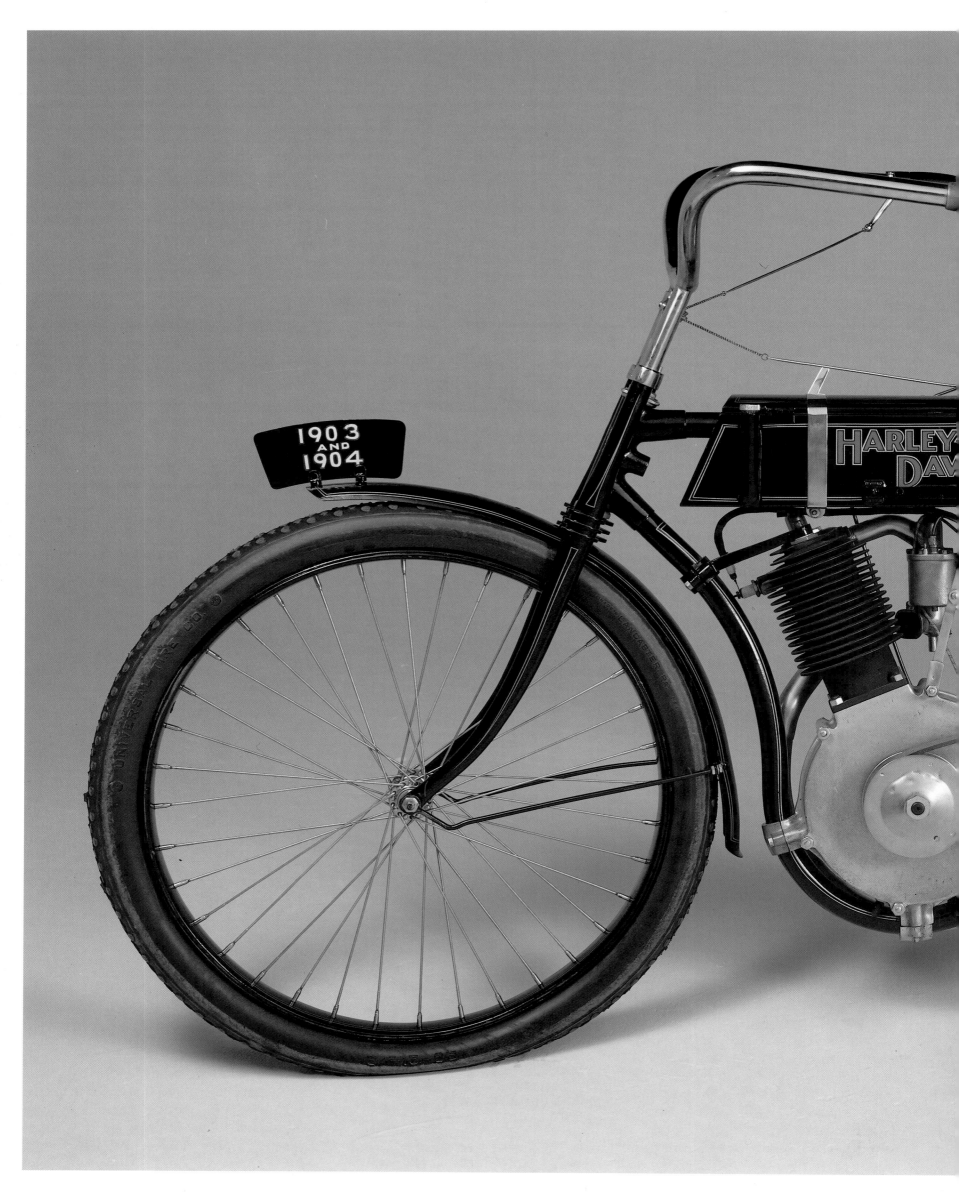

Along with one employee, they worked at their creations in a 10 ft × 15 ft (3 m × 5 m) shed built by Davidson's father in the backyard of their house at 38th and Highland Blvd. in Milwaukee, Wisconsin. (Today, the land is owned by the Miller Beer Co.!) Another non-paid employee was Aunt Janet Davidson who hand-painted the red striping on those first few motorcycles. She also created the logo soon to become known round the world, the Harley-Davidson Motor Company, seen on the fuel tanks.

One of the big improvements was the upgrading of the older style 'soup can' carburettor with an 'auto float feed' unit that, according to the sales brochure of the time, promised to allow the engine to run effortlessly from 5 to 45 mph (8 to 72 km/h) without any adjustment. That was quite an improvement at the time. It's probable that one of the Davidson neighbours, Ole Evinrude, gave them

The modernisation of the old 'soup can' carburettor with an 'auto float feed' unit proved to be a great improvement.

Technical Specification

- Engine: De Dion type, four-stroke aircooled single, approx. 25 cu. in (400cc), 3bhp;
- Lubrication: via sight feed (gravity oiler); two quarts (2.3 l);
- Ignition: via pedal actuation or by crank (3 dry cell batteries, one coil provides current);
- Carburettor: automatic float feed;
- Transmission: none, direct belt drive, handgrip throttle control.

---

the right tips on carburettor improvements. Evinrude himself went on to fame as a builder of marine engines.

Naturally, these early models were made completely by hand. They may seem primitive as they had no transmission, instead a leather belt was hooked up directly from the engine to the rear wheel rim. Forget about an electric starter or even a kick starter. You pushed the bike up to compression, jumped on, and pedalled the bicycle pedals until the engine came to life. For the price of a motorcycle that went about as fast as you could walk, you also received a bonus of plenty of healthy exercise.

The bottom line was that H-D soon took on a reputation for reliability, and over the years that followed, a special mystique that produced motorcycling magic. Magic that grows, along with the H-D motorcycles, more powerful every day.

King of the Highway
1948 Panhead

The 1948 Panhead with redesigned lifters and cylinder heads.

World War II had been over for three years and the U.S. was still basking in the glow of victory, not to mention becoming the number one world power. Hostilities had heated up the technological revolution and American industry was in the forefront. Harley-Davidson had also weathered the uncertain war years and had made considerable progress.

For example, in 1940, just prior the U.S. entrance into the war, new aluminium heads became standard for the '61' and an option for the '45' and '75' models. The next year saw the introduction of the mighty new 75 cu. in. (1200cc) overhead valve model. But Pearl Harbor sank commercial sales, at least temporarily, as the H-D plant went on wartime overdrive. H-D spent the war years building over 90,000 WLA 45's (and parts for 30,000 more), and the uniquely designed twin horizontally-opposed 45 cu. in. XA built for desert duty against Rommel, the XA sporting a shaft drive instead of the more vulnerable chain drive. However, only 1,000 of the XA's were produced, soon eclipsed by Harley's next evolution in design.

Full-scale civilian production got back into gear by 1947, and it was the all-new pushrod hydraulic valve lifter and aluminium head-equipped '74' that signalled a new era. Introduced in 1948, it also trumpeted a new name, the 'Panhead', inspired by the redesigned rocker arms and cylinder heads. Panheads took over from the previous Knuckleheads and gave their owners

The Panheads improved the oil system and were much lighter than earlier designs.

better oil systems and lighter weight, a full 8lbs (3.6 kg) lighter than the all-iron Knuckle motors.

'Pans' kept rolling off the assembly line for 18 years, quite a considerable life span. Thanks to the motor's re-markable dependability over the many years of its production, non-engine improvements received the most at-tention, including the addition of front hydraulic and rear spring suspension. Reliability and handling benefitted from improved heat dissipation and lighter overall engine weight which came about due to an increased use of aluminium in many upper-end parts.

This particular red model, a 1948 FL, still sports the sprung front end which was replaced the following year by the hydraulic set-up (on the Hydra Glide). The luxurious ride afforded by the new front end gave rise to the 'King of the Highway' title earned by the Panhead. In 1965 (as the Electra Glide), the breed

1965 saw the introduction of an electric starter and a 12 volt system (Electra Glide).

was further refined by the addition of an electric starter and 12 volt electrics.

The Panhead was really new . . . new aluminium heads, new camshaft, new exhaust ports and pipes, new intake manifold, a new oil pump (25% more oil delivery to the head), and broader heat range spark plugs which gave better low end performance. The transmission was hand operated, and the harder you threw the lever, the better the gears shifted. The clutch was foot operated, and now you pushed rather than pulled for gear changes. For its introduction in 1948, the Panhead was also offered in an optional shocking Azure Blue colour. Other additions to the basic machine included a steering head lock and a more comfortable latex-filled seat.

Technical Specification

- Engine: 45° V-Twin, aircooled, $3\frac{7}{16}$ in (87 mm) bore, $3\frac{31}{32}$ in (101 mm) stroke, 74 cu. in (1200cc) capacity, 50 bhp at 4,800 rpm;
- Lubrication: dry sump, 4 quart (4.5 l) oil tank;
- Ignition: battery;
- Carburettor: Schebler $1\frac{5}{16}$ in (33 mm);
- Transmission: 4-speed, hand gear change, foot clutch.

In 1949, besides the hydraulic front end, the Panhead took on a beefier front drum brake. In 1950 a new port design pumped up ten more horsepower, while in 1952 the first foot-shifted model was introduced.

Many changes would follow through almost two decades of production, but the heart of the Panhead remained the same dependable motor, earning it a well-deserved reputation as King of the Road.

A typical 1953 Panhead.

Spring Fever 1958
The First Sportster

A slim look and unbelievable power; the Sportster had it all.

In 1957, things were simpler, easier to understand. Television was in black and white and you could usually tell the good and bad guys by the colour of the hats they wore. Dwight D. Eisenhower was still President of the United States, and things were quiet. Then Sputnik was launched into orbit and the space race was on. And if that wasn't startling enough, along came the Sportster.

An advertisement of 1958 says 'Spring Fever – 365 days of the Year'. That's what it felt like to ride the new Sports-ter from Harley-Davidson. 'Cat-quick acceleration blends into a smooth, effortless purr – thanks to the big 55 cu. in. (883cc) OHV engine. Here is puls-ing power perfectly engineered to obey your every command'. The ad also mentions 'cloud-cushioned comfort' thanks to the hydraulic front forks and swinging-arm rear suspension. And don't forget the 'giant brakes' that 'stop you smoothly, safely'.

Maybe such phrases as 'perfect, cloud cushioned, and giant' were the ad writer's exuberance carrying him away, but there was no doubt that the Sportster's introduction marked a major new chapter in the history of the motorcycle in general and of Harley-Davidson in particular.

First introduced in 1957 (model year 1958) to replace the flathead 55-inch KH, the new overhead valve XL Sportster soon earned the rightful title of 'The Original American Muscle Bike'. It had all the right stuff, lean and mean with real 'get up and grunt' pulling power. The following year it took on its easily identifiable visual trademark, the famous 'peanut' gas tank, and a hotter cam to boot. The 'Sporty' was an instant hit and a major financial success. You don't get more American than a Sportster.

While the Sportster's predecessor, the Model K, had many good points, the new Sportster basically blew it away. The increase in displacement with the overhead valves meant 12% more horsepower. It added up to 883cc's of

Characteristics of the Sportster: the 'peanut' tank and a 'fast' camshaft.

motor and handfuls of pulse-pounding torque. OK, there was a bit of vibration, but so what. You had your hands on 40 brake horsepower and a modernised, user-friendly machine with a unit engine and transmission (you could now work on the tranny simply by removing a cover). The automotive-type rear shock absorbers smoothed out the ride to the point that the XL's were even characterised as on- and off-road machines.

Things went fast for the Sportster in more ways than one. In 1959, its second model year, it benefited from even more go-fast engineering thanks to higher-compression domed pistons, better ports, larger valves and aluminium tappets. But it was the original model that started it all, like the black and white beauty shown here.

In that 1958 ad, it also says 'Make a Date With a Sportster'. And like your first date, everybody remembers a Sportster somewhere in their life. Maybe it's TV shows like 'Then Came Bronson' (1969–70) that helped secure the indelible image of the Sportster. More likely it was the other way around, since the Sportster appeared in 1958. This TV show, starring a Sportster, was the end result of yet another person, a writer or a producer, remembering what Sportsters were all about. America, the land of apple pie and Harleys.

Technical Specification

- Engine: 55 cu. in. (833cc) air-cooled V-Twin, OHV, bore 3 in. (76 mm), stroke 3 $\frac{13}{16}$ in. (97 mm), aluminum alloy high dome pistons, 40 bhp;
- Lubrication: circulating with gear-type pressure pump and scavenger pump;
- Ignition: two-brush generator, storage battery, spark coil;
- Carburettor: Linkhert;
- Transmission: H-D four-speed, constant mesh, foot shift, hand clutch.

Last of the Breed
The 1965 Panhead

The last Panhead with the latest improvements.

In 1965 Cassius Clay (Mohammed Ali) floored Sonny Liston in 48 seconds of the first round of their boxing match, quite a shock for Sonny and also the general public. Equally surprised was the Harley public when the Harley-Davidson Motor Co., a privately held corporation for more than 60 years, went public, in a move which would lead, four years later, to a merger with the American Machine and Foundry Co., best known for making bowling pins (the dreaded AMF decal still evokes shudders from H-D traditional-

ists). On a more positive note, George Roeder gained fame by riding a tiny 15¼ cu. in (250cc) H-D Sprint to 177.225 mph (285 kph) to take the quarter litre Land Speed Record.

1965 saw another milestone passed with the production of the very last Panhead. Like the Knucklehead, it too had a long and proud reign, but had been surpassed by technology. However, 'Pans' were being continually improved, right up to the last hours of production. Now called the Electra Glide, it took on an electric starter for the first time and switched from a 6 to a 12-volt system. In addition to more zap and push-button ease of starting, the last Panheads also received an enclosed primary chain and a 5-gallon

The 1965 Panheads were called Electra Glide because of the electrical starter.

'turnpike' tank for non-stop long rides.

Introduced in 1948, the Panhead had been transformed through a long series of changes and improvements, mainly to the suspension, and reflected by changes in name. It began life with a Hardtail frame with nothing but the seat springs to smooth out the bumps. The 1949 Hydra Glide introduced hydraulics to the front end, but new levels of ride comfort were achieved by the 1958 Duo Glide. This saw the end of the hard-tail frame and the addition of a rear swinging arm and hydraulic front end. There were some initial problems with the new setup (the California Highway Patrol wanted the old hardtails back), but they were eventually solved to such a degree that aircraft manufacturers consulted H-D regarding the design of landing gear. Once again Harley-Davidson proved that they had the right stuff. 1965 saw the addition of an electric starter, and a

new name – the Electra Glide. For a while, Pans were available in both 61 and 74 cu. in. (1000 and 1200cc) displacements. Horsepower increases came with the years, ten more in 1950, and 12% more in 1956 with the addition of hi-lift cams and a better breathing air filter.

There were various designations for the last Panheads (Model 65 – FLHFB, FLFB, FLB) and all were powered by the classic 74-inch OHV motor, available in both foot and handshift. During its 18 years of production, the Pan had rightfully earned the title 'King of the Highway', and the last 6,930 F

series produced in its final year are among the many that still ply the highways and byways of the world.

The Panhead pictured here was found at a swap meet and its odometer read 45,000 original miles (72,405 km). While an English journalist once described Harleys as 'mighty Wurlitzers', the classic Pan made beautiful music with its fishtail pipes, miles of chrome, fringed solo seat, whitewall tyres and coloured matched travel luggage . . . the epitome of luxury two-wheeling.

Technical Specification

- Engine: 45° V-Twin, aircooled, 74 cu. in. (1200cc) displacement, 65 bhp;
- Lubrication: dry sump;
- Ignition: 12 volt electric start;
- Carburettor: Schleber;
- Transmission: 4-speed, handchanged or footchange optional.

1952 Cop Bike

A 1952 Harley–Davidson Panhead police bike, also called a Hydra Glide.

Way back when getting in deep trouble meant going 65 mph (105 km/h) in a 30 mph (50 km/h) zone, American cops usually rode on Harley-Davidsons or Indians. Heavy machines which are capable of idling for long periods without overheating and of motoring for hours at, for those days, high speeds of 55–65 mph (88–105 km/h). In those days the police rider was equipped with a one-way radio that could only receive and not transmit, but the motorcycle policeman could still be sent to the correct location by a dispatcher at the police department.

Police agencies first recognized the advantage of the motorcycle as early as 1904, when the first two wheeled 'motorbikes' began to appear in quantity. Indian, Harley-Davidson, Thor, Henderson, Ace and many other brands of motorcycles were used by hundreds of municipal and county traffic control jurisdictions.

The photographs show you a superb Harley-Davidson Panhead police bike from 1952. Panhead is the nickname riders gave this type of engine because of the rocker covers, which resemble pans. Another common name given is Hydra Glide, so-called because of the

front fork with hydraulic dampening, first used in 1949. The Hydra became the Duo Glide in 1958 by the addition of rear suspension.

In 1965, the last year of Panhead production, the Duo Glide was renamed Electra Glide when it received an electric starter. The Panhead came after the Knucklehead and was Harley's first overhead-valve engine, with aluminium cylinder heads and hydraulic units. The hydraulic units served to keep a zero valvelash and needed no maintenance after initial adjusting. In the first years the hydraulic units were fitted, they were at the top of the pushrods.

In 1953, because of oilfeed/pressure problems, the units of the 74 cu. in (1200cc) models were located in the lifters. The 61 cu. in (1000cc) models were only equipped with the units at the top of the pushrods. Obviously the factory did not think it was worthwhile to modify this model, because production was due to stop in 1954. The units stayed the same until 1984, the last year of the Shovelhead. In the Evolution, the units are still placed in the lifters.

The 74 cu. in (1200cc) bikes had oil for the heads fed through a hole in the cylinders. The result of this was that by the time the oil reached the head it was very hot and as thin as water, which didn't enhance cooling and lubrication very much. In 1963 the factory changed this design, oil was fed from an outside line, although the original holes were used to drain the oil from the heads. The Panhead shown has the full original police equipment in place, as it was used in those years. The bike has been restored and is an accurate reflection of how a County Sheriff's bike looked when it was delivered by the factory. By the late 1950's, American motorcycles were still the 'King of the Highway' and police agencies were buying Harleys. Indians were on the way out, although the New York Police Department used them a bit longer owing to their vast quantity of bikes and parts. In 1959 the NYPD started to phase in Harleys as the Indians began to wear out and the parts were eventually used up.

A Harley destined for law enforcement comes equipped with options not available on a civilian bike. A heavy duty generator supplied the above-

The oil is pumped into the cylinders through separate pipes.

average electrical needs of the radio and police lights. The generator is air-cooled by means of an internal fan driven by, and at the end of, the generator's armature. A big airscoop feeds the fan with air. Sparkplug wire cables were endowed with special antistatic covers to prevent radio interference.

The extra large 'police' battery is so big the oiltank had to be mounted at the outside of the frame. The original horseshoe tank was not used because of this. A first-aid kit is mounted on the top of the rear fender. At the left side of the fender is a box for police paper work and at the right side is a radio. This particular radio is a simple receiver/transmitter, with the microphone clipped to the dash. The fan-type siren is driven by the rear tire and is activated by pushing a pedal with your heel. The shaft of the siren is pushed against the tire, and makes a whole lot of noise when used at a reasonable speed.

In Europe there were several Liber-

A Harley adapted for police work has a more powerful generator.

ators and other civilian bikes equipped with a siren, but in the States this is strictly forbidden. The rest of the bike is basically the same as a civilian model, including the toolbox and the 'mousetrap'. This last part is not original on this model. The mousetrap is a mechanism that assists clutching when switching from foot to hand operated clutch. It enlarges the movement of the handclutch lever, creating enough movement of the gear box release-arm

to release the clutch as reliably as a foot-clutch.

Later this mechanism was deleted, and a shorter release-arm was used to get the correct leverage. Because a shorter release-arm needs more power to operate, they used lighter clutch springs. Feathering the clutch with the mousetrap was not so easy, and adjusting the mechanism was rather complicated because it also made use of a strong

A rack with the radio hangs on the left hand side of the bike.

spring which helped to lighten the pull of the handlebar lever. 'Mousetrap eliminator kits' are available. These kits consists of a clutch lever, a long cable with a support bracket to mount on the tube between the engine and the gearbox, and a shorter release-arm.

This example shows the beautiful tank emblems which set off the fine lines of the bike even more. These are sheetmetal stampings and not cheap plastic junk. This H-D from 1952 is a fine example of a strong machine capable of withstanding a lot of abuse.

The beautiful tank emblem was pounded out of a steel plate.

Bellowing Yellow
98 Cubic Inch Custom

This custom Harley was built by Woody Thompson of Haw River, North California.

It's natural for man to put his mark on things, be it for better or for worse. The custom motorcycle phenomena touches all kinds of machines, from 3 cu. in (50cc) mini-bikes to V-8 auto powered behemoths, but none so much as the Harley-Davidson. Personalised seems a better word than customised, because when you see a Harley that's far from stock, you can see one individual's very personal vision in three dimensional, ground shaking awesomeness.

When you trace the roots of the custom Harley you might think of Marlon Brando in the film 'The Wild One' (except he rode a Triumph) or Peter Fonda and Dennis Hopper riding 'choppers' in 'Easy Rider'. Who built the first custom Harley? Nobody knows for sure. Maybe a guy in Milwaukee who first added a couple extra running lights or leather fringe to his handlebars. Customising has come a long way since then. Today, various bike shops specialise in the fabrication of often very expensive custom Harleys emblazoned with brilliantly coloured paint schemes and layers of chrome, or

even gold plating. Still others are affectionately hammered out on a meagre budget at home.

This particular custom Harley was built by Woody Thompson of Haw River, North Carolina. Now Haw is pretty close to 'hawg', the term often applied to Big Twin Harleys. And this really is a big Twin, the Shovelhead displacing 98 cubic inches (1600cc) of pumped horsepower. Although called a '66, technically it has no real year of manufacture since the parts are a jumble of bits and pieces accumulated over time, then patiently pieced together. For instance, the '65–'66 frame was dug out of a swap meet parts pile. It was soon stuffed full of a big-bore Sidewinder 98 cubic inch (1600cc) Delcron combination. A front end was put together from various pieces including stock 2-inch (51 mm) extended Lowrider forks, while the body work including the stock Super-Glide gas tank was

A genuine Big Twin, a full 98 cubic inches (1600cc) of horsepower.

turned over to artist Teresa Crane who sprayed it golden yellow. Even the cylinder barrels were treated to an unusual choice of colour. You wouldn't call it mellow yellow, because when this bike lights up, you can feel the power all the way up into your fillings.

Built to drag racing specs by performance expert Rick Doss, 'Bellow Yellow' also sports a variety of aftermarket custom and race-oriented components, including Mackey heads, Sifton cams, S&S pistons, a Drag Specialities speedometer, and 40-inch (1016 mm) drag pipes. All that shiny stuff was chrome dipped by the Kentucky kings of glitter, Brown's Plating, probably the most famous motorcycle plating company in the world. To keep things modern and dependable, an electronic ignition feeds the spark, while Avon and Dunlop rubber take up traction

chores with MGA brakes slowing the streetster down from its fast launches.

This custom Harley has visited Daytona Beach, Florida for the annual motorcycle extravaganza known as Bike Week, when literally tens of thousands of bikes, mostly Harleys, show up for the sun and fun and racing. This 98-inch yellow thunderbolt was one of the hits of the get together, attracting crowds wherever it prowled.

Technical Specification

- Engine: 45° V-Twin, aircooled, lots of horsepower, displacement 98 cu. in (1600cc);
- Lubrication: dry sump, separate oil tank;
- Ignition: electronic;
- Carburettor: S&S;
- Transmission: 4-speed, foot-changed.

Willie G's First
1971 Super Glide

The new FX Super Glide: a combination of Big V-Twin power and the Sportster front end.

They call 1970–1980 the AMF years, the decade during which Harley–Davidson was owned by American Machine and Foundry. Most traditional Harley fans don't look favourably on those years. Maybe it had to do with the AMF 'bowling ball' decal that began 'gracing' the H-D gas tanks. Maybe it seemed the real Harley people had been pushed aside by the bigger company. It's all a matter of personal perspective. Some good things did happen. For one, money was injected into the Harley-Davidson Motor Company, something they needed very much . . . it was called 'resources for continued growth and evolution'. If you consider the fact that in 1972, under AMF leadership, the new all-alloy engined XR-750 took the racing world by storm, smashing records right and left and leaving the competition eating dust, you could say AMF control had some positive benefits.

In fact, Harley people were still very much at work even if they wore AMF/

CAUTION
DO NOT CONNECT OR
DISCONNECT PLUG
ENGINE IS

Harley t-shirts. Going aggressively after the heavy-weight custom and touring market, in 1971 they brought out the new FX Super Glide, a blending of Big V-Twin power and the Sportster's front end. The Super Glide was another milestone for the H-D Company as well as for the motorcycling world at large. It was designed by no less than Willie G. Davidson. Willie G, as he is known, was the son of the original president of H-D, William 'Bill' Davidson, and the grandson of the H-D Company's founder.

The Super Glide was Willie G's first creation and one that had long lasting effects, for it was the first of the 'factory customs', the term itself created as a result of the bike's introduction. Besides putting another word into motorcycle language, Willie G's Big Twin was actually a radical departure from its contemporaries ... and a major success.

It was a synthesis of mechanical and aesthetic thought, and it was a real groundbreaker. It featured the nimble-looking aluminium forked front end of an X-series Sportster married to the hulking F-series 74 inch Big Twin engine. The radical 'boat-tail' rear seat section was almost sci-fi in look. Some liked it, some didn't. The same went for the optional red, white and blue all-American paint scheme. But those were just details; overall, Willie G.'s Super Glide was the right bike at the right time.

Willie G. had seen the writing on the motorcycle wall. While most customisers had been plying their trade by reworking Sportsters, the new Shovelhead motor and FL frame had attracted their attention. Here was fertile ground for customising. Builders were tacking on wild extended front ends to their Shovelheads, especially radical in California. Getting a jump on the new custom movement, the Super Glide was born just in time for a whole new type of rider, the cruiser. The motorcycling world would never be the same again.

Besides looking good, it ran well. It was easy to kick-start, the transmission was super tough, and the clutch was hailed by the bike press as being about the best in the world. Better yet, the Super Glide weighed 70 pounds (32 kg) less than the FL which meant it was

The FX Super Glide sported a massive F-series 74 cu. in (1,200cc) engine.

both a low-speed chugger and a red-light rocket ship, the best of both worlds.

Willie G.'s ingenious design set off a new wave of motorcycling that subsequently produced all manner of factory customs, from the Low Rider and the Fat Bob to the Super Glide II. You begin to understand why Harley-Davidson is still around while the

other 100-odd American motorcycle companies are now just history, and why H-D continues to carve new chapters in the hopefully never ending story.

Technical Specification

- Engine: 45° V-Twin, aircooled, 60 bhp, 74 cu. in. (1200cc) displacement;
- Lubrication: dry sump, separate oil tank;
- Ignition: battery and coil, electric start and kickstart;
- Carburettor: Tillotson diaphragm;
- Transmission: 4-speed, foot shifted.

Ultra Long
Radical and Streetable '75 Sporty

Some experimental custom bike designs look good on the drawing board or even on the showroom floor, but turn out to be an exercise in futility when actually piloting one down the street. However, in the case of this radically designed, supercharged Sportster, form still does follow function ... it's seen action at both Daytona Bike Week and the annual Sturgis,

Mal Ross worked 16 hours a day, 7 days a week, for 11 weeks to produce this revolutionary 'Sporty'.

North Dakota, monster Harley meet, so it goes as well as it shows.

Mal Ross of the Parts Bin custom shop located in Spring Valley, New York,

aims at building bikes you won't see anywhere else. He designs and fabricates his unique custom bikes sparingly (4–8 per year) and with great attention to detail, handbuilding the machines from scratch, often cutting parts from blocks of raw aluminium. While he's built eight other 'blower' bikes, this particular excursion into radical bikedom is extra special.

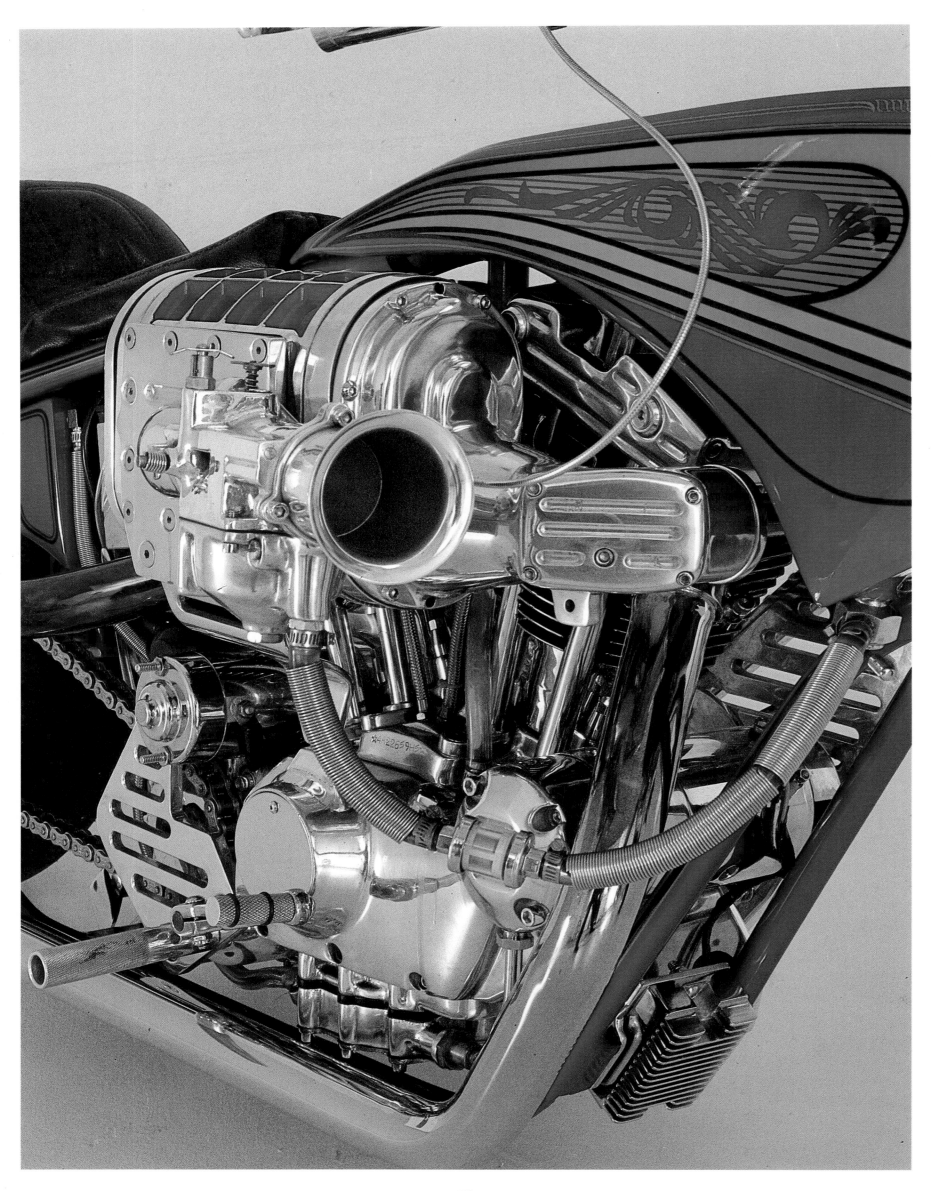

As Mal says, 'The whole bike is tricked to death'. That's an understatement when one considers this multiple show winning Harley began life as a fairly average 1975 Sportster. It racked up lots of miles with various owners before being transformed by Mal, who, inspired by the intricacies of the bike design, spent sixteen hours a day, seven days a week for seventy-seven straight days to complete the project.

While the 61 cu. in. (1000cc) Sportster motor is basically stock, it was given the bullet proof treatment, the bottom end welded, then blue printed and balanced. For added launchability, Mal bolted on a Magnuson supercharger that produces 5 lbs (2.27 kg) of boost. The boost is adjustable via a small sneeze valve located at the bottom of the intake manifold, and by changing the pulley tension. Mal fabricated many of those blower pulleys as well as the handlebars, levers, rear struts, all the various aluminium brackets, the chain guard, primary cover, footpegs, master cylinder, front motor mounts, blower struts, the seat, even the T.I.G. welded head pipes – just about every piece of the bike. 'Nothing was store bought, except the headlight', says Mal.

Other special features include the custom built clutch made by Barnett, out of a material made to run dry (the Sportster was originally built to run wet). The stock H-D tranny cases contain high performance Andrews gears. There's so much to see on the bike that some of the details may slip by unnoticed. For instance, at the bottom of the Ness triple-treed Ceriani forks and H-D fork legs are a pair of very tasty Campagnolo brakes which originally graced the front end of a 1965 MV Augusta roadracer.

The 1990 rigid frame was built by Jody Zero who stretched the neck eight inches and raked it a radical 55 degrees. Jody also handmade the gas and oil tank. In the cosmetics department, the slick moulding and candy-red paint job was handled by Dave Perewitz (Brockton, MA) who in a special effort had the work completed in a scant 21 days, in tune with Mal's marathon labours. Although the bike seems mirror bright, there's actually very little chrome plating, everything is polished aluminum except for the cast iron cylinders which are chromed.

The bike is a long 80 inches (2 m) in wheelbase, the radical look inspired by Mal's need to build a very special bike every year for Daytona Speed Week, in this case for Daytona '90. Obviously, it was labour well spent, since the bike was awarded First Place in the Harley Show and First Place in the Rat's Hole Show. You don't get much better than that . . . except that the blown Sporty also rolled away with two more First Places at the Sturgis Bike Show, where competition is very fierce.

It's an adventure, and a gamble in radical bike design that paid off, the kind of motorcycle that could feel at home on the street or on display in an art gallery . . . beauty and the beast all in one.

Technical Specification

- Engine: 45° V-Twin, aircooled, 61 cu. in (1000cc), horsepower unknown, stock bore and stroke $3\frac{13}{16}$ in (81 mm) × $3\frac{3}{16}$ in (97 mm);
- Lubrication: dry sump;
- Ignition: custom single point;
- Carburettor: Magnuson blower with S&S;
- Transmission: 4-speed H-D, footchange.

A 1991 Sportster.

The Wild One

1989 Heritage Custom

The licence plate reads 'M Brando'. No, Marlon doesn't own it, Tony Balejos of Los Angeles does. He just liked the idea of retro-building a new Evolution Big Twin to look more like a cruiser out of the 1950's when Brando was the hottest young movie star and big whitewall-tyred Harleys ruled the roads.

Tony Balejos built this 1950's tour model, 1989 Heritage custom from a new Evolution Big Twin.

The personalised licence tag is called a 'vanity plate', a very popular item in California and in other U.S. states where local government figured the idea could make them a lot of money by catering to the, well, vanity of car and bike owners who wanted to say something special about themselves or their machine.

One glance and it's easy to see this L.A.-style custom '89 Heritage has all

The power on this Heritage was increased by mounting a new cam kit, and heavy duty springs and pushrods.

the right in the world to sport such an audacious licence plate. When you spend close to $20,000 on a motorcycle and its 'custom upgrades', you probably can afford to flash the original 'Wild One's' name as a bit of nostalgia and a form of tribute, too.

Taking a new, as in a modern, Evolution Harley, and dressing it in vintage parts, is a popular movement among custom H-D enthusiasts. You get the reliability and ease of the new higher-tech Harley plus the charm and elegance of the old-style bikes. In this case the owner came up with the

design, rather than one of the Harley 'boutique' shops catering to Hollywood stars and starlets who order up such megabuck Harleys.

Now paint is the first thing people see on a motorcycle, and makes a powerful visual statement. Colours are not chosen lightly, nor the painters . . . no, not painters, call them artists, a title richly deserved by the few master bike

painters who have been known to receive up to $5,000 for a special 'spray' job. In this case, Damon's Paint in Anaheim laid on the pink and white highlighted by mint green pinstriping. Damon's shop, complete with state-of-the-art spray booths, banks of heat lamps and a vast array of environmental safeguards, has been at the leading edge of top quality motorcycle paint for many years. Such is their level of perfection, that if a single, tiny bubble or scratch can be found, they will completely repaint the tank or fender until they get it right. It's the same level of professionalism and care that

most people involved in Harleys seem to share.

And by all accounts, Damon's got the '50s colours just right on Tony's neo-classic Heritage, the model name very appropriate in that it melds past and present, the owner's intention. Even the saddle, re-upholstered from a stock seat with the addition of a white leather insert, decorative studs, conchos, and leather fringe, recalls the golden olden days when Harleys were luxury land yachts plying the country in all directions. By all accounts, those days are back in full swing thanks to

Past and present artfully combined to achieve unbelievable beauty.

Harley riders like Tony and painters like Damon.

When deciding upon the mechanical enchantment as opposed to the cosmetics, Tony chose to install some performance upgrades in the internals of the 80 cu. in (1300cc) Evo motor. Los Angeles Harley-Davidson turned up the power band by adding a hypo cam kit, heavy duty springs and pushrods while a Screamin' Eagle carb and Paughco fishtail pipes help in the fuel

feed and breathing areas. And about that 'M Brando' licence plate . . . we don't think Marlon will mind.

Technical Specification

- Engine: 1989 Evolution 45° V-Twin, aircooled, 80 cu. in (1300cc), approx. 65 bhp.;
- Lubrication: dry sump, separate oil tank;
- Ignition: battery and coil;
- Carburettor: Screamin' Eagle;
- Transmission: H-D five speed, footshift.

Minnesota Mindbender
1989 FLSTC Heritage Custom

Bartels in Los Angeles, California, ranks high on the list of Harley-Davidson dealers and custom bike builders, and they manage to produce some very potent race machines as well. The shop, actually located in Culver City, a 'suburb' of the sprawling L.A. megalopolis, caters to a wide variety of customers, including a large number of celebrities, movie stars, tele-

Kevin Olson's flashy FLSTC Heritage Custom. He wanted a change from his simple black Harley.

vision personalities, and rock musicians, many of whom are more or less recently caught up in the Harley mystique. They need a Harley to cruise Beverly Hills or the avant-garde Melrose Boulevard or to rumble in mini-packs down Sunset Boulevard on a

warm Sunday morning on their way to brunch at Spago's.

Maybe it was Bartels that started a major new wave of Harley riders, at least in the L.A. area. Needless to say some serious money went into these Hollywood Harleys since many of the riders were very image conscious in the most image conscious city in the

overseas dealer in Osaka, Japan, where the roadracer's unique frame was designed and built. Roger and Arnie, builders of 'double your fun, double your horsepower' Harleys, are dialing in the extra horsepower the Evo Sportster powerplant needs to compete against the heavy hitters from Ducati,

This radical racer is made from aluminium, titanium and magnesium.

Moto Guzzi and other such European roadracers.

The 74 cu. in (1200cc) Sportster-based engine will take on a specially de-

signed 8500 rpm crankshaft which will be the key to the extra helpings of horsepower. Roger and Arnie say they are 'looking for a safe redline of 8,000 rpm.' The legendary headwork specialists at C.R. Axtell will be lashing the motor to the dyno as they develop the new head which could be a two valve

with castings, the components were machined from solid T6 billet stock and then hollowed out on a mill. Costly? You could say so. A ballpark figure for the frame alone runs about twenty grand.

And when you consider that the radical road burner is fashioned from aluminium, titanium and magnesium, the Yen count rises dramatically. The Dymag wheels are magnesium and all the major hardware, rear sets, through-bolts and axles are hewn from titanium. The Robocop body parts are fabricated from feather-light, tank-tough carbon fibre.

Dripping wet the bike tips the scales at a mere 320lb (145 kg), much lighter than even the mid-size Japanese pocket rockets. When you figure in 120 horsepower at the rear wheel in final trim, you're talking serious power to weight advantages.

While being tested and campaigned in the U.S., the hyper-Harley will be piloted by Doug Toland and when in Japan the reins will be turned over to a Mr. Aoki for international racing. Since it's a non-production frame, it is not eligible for production class racing, but will be battling it out in Pro Twins GP and, most likely, Classified Formula One.

This is one Harley that just might bridge the East/West gap in one flying leap.

or possibly one of the new four valve set-ups from Rivera Engineering. Ax-tell has already supplied XRV with a set of one-off, very hot solid lifter cams.

The East/West Roadracer dazzles you with science as well as the highly polished lattice-work aluminium frame. Handmade and literally cut

The frame is a technical wonder with its polished aluminium honeycomb structure.

from large blocks of aluminium, it is largely composed of oval section tubing. Some of the box sections are hand forged sheet metal, which are welded into boxes, and then welded to pieces normally made from castings. But to avoid problems of porosity associated

---

Technical Specification

- Engine: 45° V-Twin, aircooled, 74 cu. in (1200cc) displacement, 98 bhp at 6400 rpm;
- Lubrication: dry sump, separate oil tank;
- Ignition: C.D.I.;
- Carburettor: 1⁶⁄₁₀ in (40 mm) Mikuni;
- Transmission: H-D 4-speed.

New/Old Springer

When in 1949, Harley-Davidson ceased using the springer front fork on its Big-Twins, they didn't disappear, and at many dealers springer forks lay gathering dust together with other leftover parts. The fifties saw many changes in the motorcycling scene, with the notoriety of the movie 'The Wild One' featuring Marlon Brando, and because a lot of riders were chop-

The best of both worlds, old style, modern technology.

ping their Harley's to make them lighter and faster. This chopping raised a demand for alternative parts, eventually creating the aftermarket industry.

At the end of the sixties, springers of all lengths and quality became available, including some which were over half a metre longer than standard. Handling was of course affected, mostly in a negative way. But choppers were all the rage for early 1970's contemporary bikers, and to modify a bike to the style of that time demanded lots of innovation. The need for such acces-

sories gave birth to many of today's suppliers such as Drag Specialities, Custom Chrome Inc. (CCI), Paughco and others.

By the mid-70s, only the production of engines and transmissions remained at the old H-D premises, leaving the space and the potential to create new motorcycles. It took a few years before any of these efforts paid off, however. Harleys did not seem to be attractive to the new generation of bikers, and those that bought a new H-D in the 70s were mostly long-time riders of the

A 'New/Old' Springer with a totally dependable, maintenance free, Evolution engine.

type. But thanks to a styling redesign by William G. Davidson and his team of designers, sales were starting to climb. By 1981, production had risen from 14,000 in 1969 to 50,000 in 1980, and the H-D management felt strong enough to buy the company back from AMF.

Customer feedback concerning the stock models, and the way that riders

were then building their 'choppers' started to influence the factory. The chopper of the early '70s had not vanished, but had changed somewhat in appearance. Accessories were now being added to the bike to style it, although there will always be chopper purists who think that every unnecessary part is extra weight and 'undesirable junk'. In response to many enthusiasts re-using the springer front ends, the factory designed a new springer for some Evolution models, adapted to modern technology and the demands of today's riders.

The modern springer has a fork-knife connection at the legs and the rockers, so the legs won't bend under load. The rocker bearings have teflon liners and are adjustable. The springers do not stick like telescopic forks sometimes do when braking (caused by the friction of oilseals and bushings). The new springer was presented as a limited edition of 1,500 in June 1989, and all were sold before the end of the year.

The new fork is shown on the bike in the photographs, which has the best of both worlds – old style with the ease of modern technology such as an electric starter, five speed gearbox, disc brakes,

A Softail Springer with a 21 in (533 mm) front wheel and high handlebars.

a Softail frame with 'hidden' suspension and, of course, the ultra-reliable and maintenance-free Evolution engine. The rear belt is neatly hidden under the genuine leather saddlebags, which keeps the rear end clean and maintenance-free. Originally this was an FXSTS, a stock 1989 Softail Springer. It has, as clearly can be seen, undergone the necessary changes to get the classic look. The dash has been

changed for one with three lights from CCI, and the use of the original style handlebars from V-Twin adds to the nostalgic look. Tail light, horn, headlight, front fenderlight and exhaust pipes are also CCI. The seat is stock. The nice paint scheme and the original H-D bags enhance the classic look, the 'tombstone' tail light gives the rear a definitive old appearance. This tail light was stock on the Knuclehead and some Panheads. Old looking exhaust and bags complete the picture. Colours are white, grey and burgundy, with stripes. The whole thing has been done by Kennedy's Custom Cycle in Oceanside, California.

Stealth Bike

This magnificent Stealth Bike was constructed from a 1987 Heritage Softail.

The owner of this creation wanted a bike that has the looks and power to match his riding style. Which is why he commissioned Burchinal Performance of Anaheim, California (USA), to build it for him.

This custom builder was given a budget and a schedule to keep to. The bike was finished long before they ran

out of time and costs were exactly the available budget.

He started with a 1987 Heritage Softail which got the full treatment. Everything got painted black or chromed

and most of the stock parts got replaced with custom parts.

The engine was completely rebuilt. It got an S&S lower end consisting of balanced flywheels with a longer stroke of $4\frac{5}{8}$ in (117 mm), and new S&S pistons which match the flywheels. Displacement is 90 cu. in (1400cc) and the compression ratio has gone up

from the stock 8.5 to 1, to 9.25 to 1.

S&S also takes care of carburation by means of the indestructable 1⅞ in (29 mm) Super B. Stock ignition has been replaced by points and a Dyna coil. The advantage of this is that there is no rev limiter, because when the engine reaches 5200 revs this retards the igni-

The front end sports Burchinals triple trees and 2 in (51 mm) longer forks for the ultimate custom look.

tion timing to 0 thus reducing power. A disadvantage is that the points and advance mechanism need relatively high maintenance.

Cylinder heads are treated to Burchin-

als 'in house' modifications, and an Andrews camshaft has been used with the stock hydraulic lifters. This camshaft was chosen because it would make a good combination with the Drag Specialities Python Pipes.

This exhaust system has an especially good low end performance because of

had been cut up and the parts massaged into a one-off frame. Besides being shortened for an ultra low profile, the frame was then powder coated and the Sportster tank painted 'Hi-Ho Silver'. A pair of spun aluminium Mitchell wheels were mounted, complete with Dunlop 391 rubber.

Into the frame was stuffed a '72–73 vintage Shovelhead motor pumped up to 91 cu. in (1500cc) with a 3¾" (95 mm) stroke and stock bore with 9.75:1 compression. Renowned top end specialist Dave Mackey worked his magic which included dual plug conversion and stainless steel valves operated by a hot Leinweber cam. Standard unleaded pump gas is all that's required, the fuel fed via an S&S 'D' carb. A Morris magneto with a Morris trigger unit fires the coils separately, basically a dual ignition system. As a result, it's a 'one-kick' operation to start the bike.

The 4-speed H-D tranny was built up to match the increased demands of the hyper motor but again is composed of the 'left over parts' including an early ratchet top, late gears, late shaft, early slider clutches, the whole package then geared 3.09 and connected to a ¾ inch (19 mm) belt drive unit.

As a show bike it was street legal and actually an extremely quick handling machine due in part to its low weight, 420 lbs (191 kg). At 130 mph (210 km/h) the bike tracks straight and true without any effort.

Though tuned to run on Los Angeles freeways, the guys at Jammer were curious to see how well the bike could run at the top end of the spectrum. What better place to test the performance of the Junkyard Dog than at the famous Bonneville Salt Flats, where land speed records had been set and broken for decades.

The bike was loaded up and hauled off to Bonneville, and then without any further rejetting and carb work, the Junkyard Dog was set loose on the salt flats. It was going to be raced like it was ridden on the L.A. street, without any modifications or special tuning. The best run was a healthy 135.7 mph (218 km/h), and it was going faster on another run when the belt broke. Currently the bike is being updated for another attack on the Bonneville speed records.

Technical Specification

- Engine: 45 V-Twin, aircooled, 85 bhp, stock bore, 3¾" (95 mm) stroke, 91 cu. in (1500cc) displacement;
- Lubrication: dry sump, separate oil tank;
- Ignition: Morris magneto and trigger, dual system;
- Carburettor: S&S 'D';
- Transmission: 4-speed 'left over parts'.

Another radical chopper with an Evolution engine.

Classic Hardtail
Jammer '91 Custom Evolution

Jammer Cycle Parts, Inc. is one of the longest running stories in the annals of custom Harley-Davidsons, the company tracing its roots back to 1968 when it was known as D&D Distributors, operating out of Burbank, California. Then it became 'Psychedelic Choppers' and finally Jammer in 1971, when they moved to nearby Glendale, CA. President M.C. Blair and Vice-

Everything on this bike is custom made, with the exception of the new 80 cu. in. (1300cc) Evolution engine.

President E.Z. Winarsky live, ride, breathe and occasionally sell custom-built Harleys as well as stay very busy as distributors for H-D custom and speed equipment.

M.C., himself involved for over 25

years in motorcycling, rode a 1947 Knucklehead from his hometown in Minnesota to California in 1958, intent on escaping the cold and finding year round riding weather. Jammer Cycle Parts was the gold at the end of the California rainbow, which eventually became the centre for custom bike design. Jammer now builds 10–12 bikes a year on special order.

Besides building special order Harleys and supplying every kind of part, Jammer has also been involved in designing and building racing bikes. Their Harley powered streamliner recently rocketed to 322 mph (518 km/h) at Bonneville Salt Flats, earning it the much coveted title of fastest motorcycle in the world.

A combination of 19 in (483 mm) Avon and 16 in (406 mm) Michelin tyres gives this bike all the grip it needs. The brakes are by Performance Machine.

This particular 1991 hardtail custom features some of that special performance pedigree. Everything on the bike, except the brand new 4-speed 80-inch

Evolution motor, is custom, Jammer custom in fact. The 65 horsepower motor took on a hotter street cam, prepped and polished headwork, an SU 1⅞ in (48 mm) carb, and then was nestled into one of Jammer's 'fatbob rigid' frames. It also features an H-D gearbox fitted with Andrews close ratio gears. Partial to the practicality

and strength of belt drives, Jammer bolted on a ⅓ in (8 mm) Primo unit which runs a Uniroyal belt.

The bike features both electric start and kickstart for convenience and tradition. Jammer believes a bike can be customised and easy to maintain as well, so they installed a KV electronic ignition. This particular bike is one of five built for one customer, and part of a very limited run of 20 to the same general configuration.

Although the low height and largish 5-gallon (23 l) Fatbob gas tank give the bike a massive look, the Jammer custom weighs a very respectable 520 lbs (236 kg). A combination of 19- and 16 inch (483 and 406 mm) Avon and Michelin tires are teamed up with Performance Machine brakes. Jammer has assembled a network of specialists who handle the various stages of preparation and fabrication in the complex process of building a bike from scratch. In the cosmetics department, Jammer sent the shiny parts to Van Nuys Plating for chroming, and Jim from 'Hawg Dawgs' produced the graphics.

Technical Specification:

- Engine: 45° V-Twin, aircooled, 65 bhp, 80 cu. in (1300cc) displacement;
- Lubrication: dry sump, separate oil tank;
- Ignition: KV electronic ignition;
- Carburettor: S&S 1⅞ in (48 mm);
- Transmission: 4-speed, close ratio.

El Primo Primer
Econo Custom with Class

Custom bikes are a very personal business. Beauty is in the eye of the beholder, one man's meat is another man's poison and all that stuff. In this case, 'El Primo Primer' is the very special vision of E.Z. Winarsky, Vice President of Jammer Cycle Products, Glendale, CA. While Jammer builds custom bikes for customers on a special order basis, this is E.Z.'s personal

Time and time again El Primo steals the attention from the more colourful bikes.

ride. And wherever it goes, even in Los Angeles where $30–50,000 ultra-flash Harleys are plentiful, El Primo seems to pull the crowds away from the more brightly coloured bikes. Could be its unique paint job, more likely its unique character.

It's back to basics with El Primo, where the motorcycle as machine stands out over the glitter and gloss of expensive paint and chroming. The bike looks carved from a single block of metal, and its 'tiny' low profile tyres and big fenders make it low and large at the same time. It has a classic look, too, with the matt grey set off by the touch of gleaming chrome in the old style

fishtail mufflers. Yet there is also the rough-hewn look, from the glass-beaded engine to the unadorned gas tanks.

The project began as an idea about a year before assembly started, the mocked-up bike sitting in E.Z.'s office. The final build took only three weeks after several months of contemplation.

The big rear fender is made of glass fibre.

It was not an easy job. For starters, an out of production Jammer frame was used and had to be modified to accept the later Evo engine. The frame features a 2¼ in (57 mm) stretch up front

and no rake. It's easy to see that the big Evo motor really fills up the frame, and the tank sits low, contributing to the 'stuffed full' look. The bike's clean look is aided by the old style steel lower legs. Because they use the older style damper, they're a little noisy and rough, but they are 'right' for this bike. Wide Glide triple trees round out the front end fork package.

Though not easy to detect, the large valenced rear fender is glass-fibre while the front unit is steel. Both axles roll low profile Pirelli rubber on stock earlier-style H-D mag wheels, producing a very impressive look. 4-piston Performance Machine brakes were given the black anodized caliper treatment, the over large 11½ in (292 mm) rotors fashioned from stainless steel. Again the large rotors contrasting with the small 16-inch (406 mm) wheels produces that 'stuffed full' look and makes the small wheels look even smaller. All in all, the bike tips the scales at 477 lbs (217 kg) wet.

Another trick feature figuring into the bike's clean look is the sealed 12 volt custom battery hidden from sight in the bottom of the oil tank. In addition, two Dyna coils fire each cylinder independently.

Oh, and the trick paint job. Would you believe a spray can of Krylon grey primer with a touch of matt? The source of the pinstriping we'll keep secret. It just proves ingenuity always wins out over sheer bucks.

Somehow E.Z. has mixed all the design treatments together to produce a whole greater than the sum of the parts. The bottom line is that El Primo Primer never fails to attract attention. Call it quiet understatement, call it cool confidence . . . hell, call it E.Z.'s bike.

The '91 Evo motor had its head milled 65 thousandths of an inch (1.65 mm) and was fitted with a hotter street cam, adjustable pushrods, Dyna single-fire ignition and the newly introduced S & S Super E carburettor. The Evo now pumps out 80 hp to the rear wheel.

The transmission was treated to a super duty S.T.D. alloy case housing

The 91 Evo engine was souped-up with a 'hotter' camshaft, adjustable pushrods, Dyna single fire ignition and an S&S Super E carburettor.

close ratio gears which were mated to a hydraulic clutch, while a 3-inch Phase Three belt drive and connector plate teamed up with an Atlas clutch. All the lines were custom made and plumbed.

Technical Specification

- Engine: 45° V-Twin, aircooled, 80 bhp, 80 cu. in (1300cc) displacement;
- Lubrication: dry sump, separate oil tank;
- Ignition: Dyna, independent coils;
- Carburettor: S&S Super E;
- Transmission: 4-speed, S.T.D. cases.

Supercharged Sled
Hayden Hamilton's 95-inch Softail

Hayden's first bike was a 3 cu. in (50cc) mini-bike that he bought on money saved from a paper route. Hayden's a big believer in saving, then investing. From box boy, to selling air compressors out of his apartment, to owning three beer bars by the time he was 26, his financial theory has led him from a job bagging groceries to the owner of

Hayden calls his 95 cu. in (1560cc) Softail: 'The mother of all bikes'.

14 auto-repair centres in the Los Angeles San Fernando Valley.

Some twenty years after getting off his last bike, a Triumph Bonneville, Hayden was opening up one of his

auto centres across the street from a Harley dealer. He kept walking over and checking out the new bikes. One day, he rolled away on a brand new '88 FXSTC Softail. He had the fever, he admits, and was 'hooked on Harleys.'

After puttering around on the bike, he tried various performance improve-

ments. 'I bashed out the baffles the second week,' he says. Then one day he got smoked by another Harley which had a cam and a Del Orto carb. He decided not to be beat again, and started what became a rapidly escalating series of power upgrades, finally ending up with a monster bike.

A new '88 FXSTC was rebuilt into this 95 cu. in (1560cc) Softail.

After researching all the bike mags for the best possible components, Hayden decided to go all out. He sent the motor, now with 36,000 miles (58,000 km) on the odometer, to The Motor Shop (Glendale, AZ) where the supercharger experts spent two months completely disassembling and rebuilding the Evo motor, which included blue printing, and grafting on the over-driven B&M blower with 6 pounds (2.7 kg) of boost. Engine dis-

dialing in the correct jets for the dual-throat Del Orto carb, a tricky business when you add a blower and lower the compression ratio (to 7:1). He also readjusted the blower pulleys to change the ratio from 1:1 to 1.6:1 for increased boost. As a result of the increased 'fun ratio,' he replaces his rear tire every 60 days of 'average' riding. He was also going through a clutch every three weeks until he bolted on one of Barnet's new kevlar clutches which seems to be holding up fine even with the stresses caused by 160 h.p.

The Softail runs through the gears of a stock 5-speed H-D tranny while the brakes were upgraded to Performance Machine binders. The exhaust system was switched for a Super Trapp fitted with 22 plates while hot sparks are fired through a Dyna Single Fire solid state ignition system. The stock suspension was retained with the addition of Wide Glide lower forks to take on the dual disc brakes. Astro Plating in Van Nuys laid on the gleam (including the inner primary and rear swing-arm) while Jane of Jane's Cycle Arts painted the flamed white-pearl highlighted by acid etched gold leaf.

Totally streetable, the FXSTC-B (for blower) purrs like a kitten, idles smoothly, and provides launches of warp factor proportions. Hayden's personal vision started out with 'bashed out baffles' and was transformed into what he sums up as 'the mother of all bikes.' Could be.

Chrome by Astro Plating. Paint by Jane's Cycle Arts.

placement was increased to 95 cu. in (1550cc) thanks to Sputhe cylinders. The unstroked motor also took on a re-aligned cank, S&S connecting rods, a Crane drag cam, hydraulic lifters, Sputhe pistons and Total Seal piston rings while the lower end was kept stock. S.T.D. (Chatsworth, CA) reworked the heads with their big valve kit and a dual plug per head conversion. The bike ran so fast after the headwork that Hayden thought S.T.D. had filled

his bike with race gas. Actually the bike runs just fine on pump fuel.

Since Hayden grew up working at his Dad's Shell stations, he knew how to handle a wrench, and did much of the work himself. He spent many hours

---

Technical Specification

- Engine: 45° V-Twin, aircooled, 160 bhp, 95 cu. in (1550cc) displacement;
- Lubrication: dry sump, separate oil tank;
- Ignition: Dyna Single Fire, dual plugs;
- Carburettor: Del Orto;
- Transmission: stock H-D 5-speed.

Turn Key Custom
Vic Triepke's Made to Order Ness-bike

Vic Triepke goes back a long way when it comes to custom bikes, motorised and otherwise. In the early '60s, Vic, at age 6, was already building and riding trick 'chopper' bicycles, one equipped with an extended springer front end and king and queen seat.

But as a youngster, he also enjoyed rides on his cousin's suicide shift

An '87 FXRP was transformed into this special-order knock-out cafe-style red rocket.

Harley. When he was ten, he saved up $45 and bought a Taco 22 mini-bike, and in 1967 got into motocross and desert racing. He earned factory-sponsored rides and won several

trophies racing as a pro, but retired after a backbreaking crash fazed him out of competition.

Vic's around the clock business makes him well known with motorcyclists all over Southern California. His 24 hour towing service picks up and transports bikes in need. He's come to the rescue of countless riders and has the equip-

ment to handle all kinds of machines . . . dressers, sidecar rigs, bikes with trailers, you name it. He's also known as the 'Tower to the Stars' since he has helped haul Harleys for the likes of James Caan, Sylvester Stallone, Arnold Schwarzenegger, Billy Idol and other high profile L.A. celebrities.

Ness custom parts, many made from solid aluminium, constitute most of this bike.

As far as his own riding goes, Vic got into building flat tracker-type Triumphs for the street then later on

picked up a Harley Softail and radically customised it, complete with ape hanger bars and red, white and blue paint. Deciding he wanted to make a quantum leap, he went to Arlen Ness, the premier custom bike designer, and brought home this built-to-order knock-out Ness cafe-style '87 FXRP.

Crane supplied the 286 cam and lifters. The highly polished and chromed Evo engine was bolted in an '87 FXR frame which was raked 38 degrees.

The H-D forks were shortened 2 in (51 mm) and dressed up with Ness triple clamps. Shocks are Koni units with Performance Machine brakes clamping down on an 18 in (457 mm) rear and a 21 in (533 mm) front rolling Metzler rubber. The dependable H-D 5 speed tranny was kept stock.

Most of the bike is a collection of Ness custom parts, much of it crafted from billet aluminium. The list includes bars, grips, mirrors, fenders, headlight, tail light, front and rear pegs, the seat and exhaust system. Arlen also painted the blood red paint with special art work by Ron M. From the day the order was placed to the day the paint had dried, the project took six months at Arlen's shop in San Leandro, CA.

Now this bit of self-indulgence didn't come cheap, the price tag hovering around $30,000 plus some later fine tuning. Vic gets some serious kicks from his bucks, owning one of the most outstanding rides in L.A. But he's already thinking of building his own bike, and may be relinquishing ownership of the red rocket. Hey, Stallone, Arnold . . . you need this bike.

Most people don't realize that Arlen Ness only recently began building custom bikes to customer's specifications. In the past, Arlen built a bike based on his own personal design, and if you liked it, you bought it.

The order form for this included an 89

The 'Turnkey Custom', an 89 cu. in (1460cc) engine with a complete S&S camshaft and S&S carburettor.

cu. in (1460cc) motor with an S&S lower end and S&S carb with Don Rich handling the internal balancing specs.

Technical Specification

- Engine: 45° V-Twin, aircooled, 89 cu. in (1460cc) displacement, 80 bhp;
- Lubrication: dry sump, separate oil tank;
- Ignition: Dyna;
- Carburettor: S&S;
- Transmission: Stock H-D 5 speed.

Hog Town Harley
Barry Weiss' Cowboy Custom FLH

Barry Weiss' thoroughbred. A cowboy custom FLH, a bike that stands out in a crowd.

The owner of this hand-tooled Harley's gone through about 30 bikes over the years, Triumphs, BSAs, Nortons, and Harleys, and has done his share of off-road racing including the Barstow to Vegas run, and plenty of cow trailing up fire roads out in the boonies. But he also had a soft spot for the old look of the big hawg cruisers. He's also a native Californian, having been born

and raised in Los Angeles where hot motorcycles, like sunshine, are everywhere. He wanted a Harley that would stand out in the midst of all the super-nice bikes that hung out at the local Burger stand.

Now there's nothing more American than Harley-Davidsons, unless it's cowboys. Put the two together and you've got this Hogtown flier, an FLH that really defines 'Blazing Saddles.' Barry found the bike in Nebraska with 4,300 original miles (6,900 km) on the odometer. Now everything in that neck of the woods is advertised as having been 'ridden only by a Shriner

during parades.' This one was so clean and stock, the story could have been true. Barry had the bike freshened up in Nebraska, bolting on a whole store full of after market H-D accessory items like the 'passing lights,' the axle covers and fender bumpers, with Brown's Plating handling the addition-

50s style in two-tone green and camel.

al chroming. All the parts are appropriate for the year, the bike being a 1979 FLH, the last year for the 74 cu. in. (1200cc) engine.

The bike was then shipped to California, its stock red paint shed in favour of a 'two tone' arrangement of green and camel sprayed by Spin in Costa Mesa. Barry favours the old style '50s look of the FLHs. He was also inspired by a memory as a kid growing up in Hollywood. He remembered seeing a

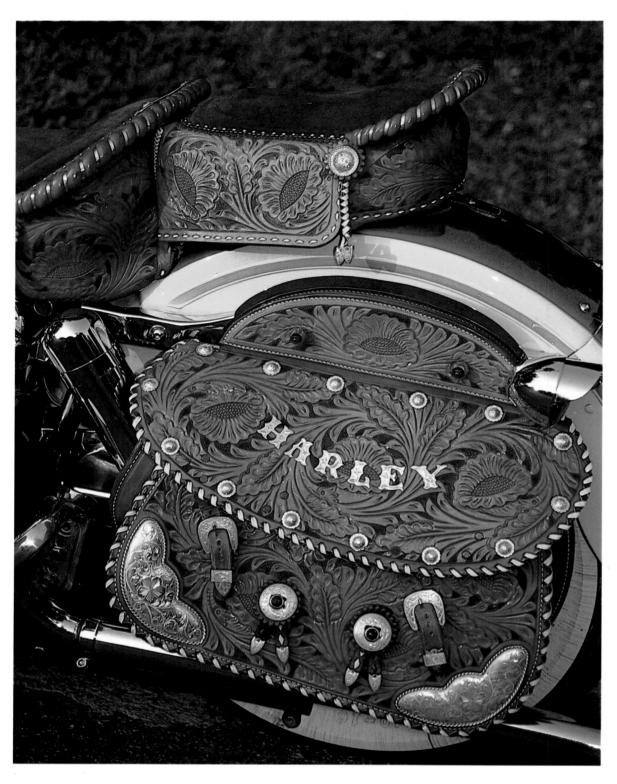

famous rodeo tailor to the stars named Noody who drove around in a Caddy Eldorado with six gun door handles and saddle leather seats. Noody also rode around on a Triumph Bonneville featuring tooled leather upholstery. Years later, the image still in his head, Barry was looking for something different for his bike. He came away with a full western saddle and bags, all hand tooled by Miguel Lepe, a premier saddle maker in L.A. The engraved and filigreed sterling silver pieces were brought from Mexico. The end product was a very rich look when combined with the white rubber footboards, pegs, and grips and the traditional green and camel paint; a look that's distinctive, something you'd remember, along with the custom licence plate, 'HOGTOWN.'

Now while Barry owns a couple Triumphs and a cafe-styled Ness Harley, he still gets plenty of enjoyment from his 'golden oldie'. He says riding the FLH is 'like riding a Maytag washing machine' and enjoys late night summer 'riding tours' round L.A. in a bike that really sits tall in the saddle.

A real western saddle with side bags complements the cowboy custom FLH.

Technical Specification

- Engine: 45° V-Twin, aircooled, 74 cu. in. (1200cc) displacement, 50 bhp;
- Lubrication:dry sump, separate oil tank;
- Ignition: stock;
- Carburettor: SU;
- Transmission: stock H-D.

'1 TOPHOG'
Tim McNalley's Hollywood Harley

Tim McNalley was about to head out to Sturgis, South Dakota for the annual big Harley rally on his '87 H-D Police Bike when a pit bull named Maude pulled him down a flight of stairs. So instead of heading out to South Dakota he passed the time detailing his FXRSP while his arm healed. Tim knows something about 'detailing' since for the past 30 years, Tim has been work-

Unique artwork with silver double letters on Tim McNalley's Hollywood Harley.

ing behind the scenes at Hollywood movie studios making the film stars look younger and better looking through the magic of make-up. He's worked on dozens of movies including Rambo 3.

Tim's Miata blue 80 cu. in (1300cc) Evo needed some final touches after just being unleashed from the San Leandro California Center for Outrageous Harleys, namely the workshop of Arlen and Cory Ness. Cory had put in 110% effort, even to the point of having the bike painted twice since the shade of blue was not quite what Tim had envisioned. The unique paint scheme

A 100 bhp engine was mounted in this bike for extra 'Pit Bull Power'.

including the silver leaf letter work was created by the paintmaster of Campbell, California, Dennis Dardinelli.

It's easy to see that this H-D's beauty isn't just skin deep as soon as you get within fifty feet of '1 TopHog.' But to put some Pit Bull power behind all the cosmetic good looks, Tim dropped the bike off with Roger and Arnie of XRV Performance Products in N. Hollywood, California.

Additions included a Crane 1000 cam, a 1.57 in (40 mm) Mikuni carb and Ramjet injector manifold, Axtell heads, and Crane adjustable pushrods plus a CHP module ignition. All said and

done, the SP left XRV pumping out a serious 100 horsepower.

Ness accessory products festoon the bike including the lights, fenders and rear struts. Triple A handled all the chrome 'show and go' pieces, while Dennis Manning of BUB fame served up the exhaust system. JB brakes and forward controls, Performance Machine wheels and a custom Mike Corbin seat round out the picture perfect Hollywood Hawg that rides a mere four inches off the ground.

Tim prowls the streets and boulevards of Hollywood with the 75 members of the Hawg Dogs, movie directors and producers, car dealers, and high rollers who share one common fantasy, owning the ultimate Harley. None of them would argue that Tim hasn't got close enough.

Technical Specification

- Engine: 45° V-Twin, aircooled 80 cu. in (1300cc), 100 bhp;
- Lubrication: Dry sump, separate oil tank;
- Ignition: Dyna;
- Carburettor: 1.57 in (40 mm) Mikuni;
- Transmission: H-D 5-speed.

Never Ending Story
1983 Shovelhead Custom

A 1983 Harley FXWG.

The first Shovelhead appeared in 1966 and continued in production until 1983, the dawn of the Evolution motor. Pictured here is the last of the lineage, an '83 vintage Harley FXWG. Most people know the FX as the Super Glide, the WG standing for Wide Glide (or maybe Will G., Vice-President of Styling). It's strong appeal lay in its low slung look and ride, the seat riding only 26¼ in (667 mm) off the ground. The lighter look was carried over to the front end by the trimmer treaded 21 inch (533 mm) front wheel and unshrouded front forks, with the smaller brake rotors and calipers also contributing to a slimmed down low, look.

One of the last Shovels, this custom with the sweet black cherry paint job belongs to Dan Baan of Mathews, North Carolina, who has seen the Wide Glide through a series of transformations. Whatever form it takes, it seems to come out a winner each time. Before it took on its present persona, it scored big at the annual Harley Ride-in Show and Rat's Hole Bike Show in

Daytona during Bike Week. Custom bike building is a never ending story, the owners rarely ever satisfied that the project is really finished down to the last stainless allen bolt. There's always something else to add. Usually a bike is 'almost finished'. In this case, the bike really was maxed out.

To emphasize the colours, the headlight is also painted instead of chromed.

So at this point, Dan could either just ride the bike, sell it and start all over again on a new project, or just tear the bike down to pieces and put the puzzle back together in a different way. It's the process of creation that keeps custom bike builders anxious to start something new just about the time they've added the last possible bell, whistle or chromed doodah to their pride and joy. Like all artists they are only happy when working.

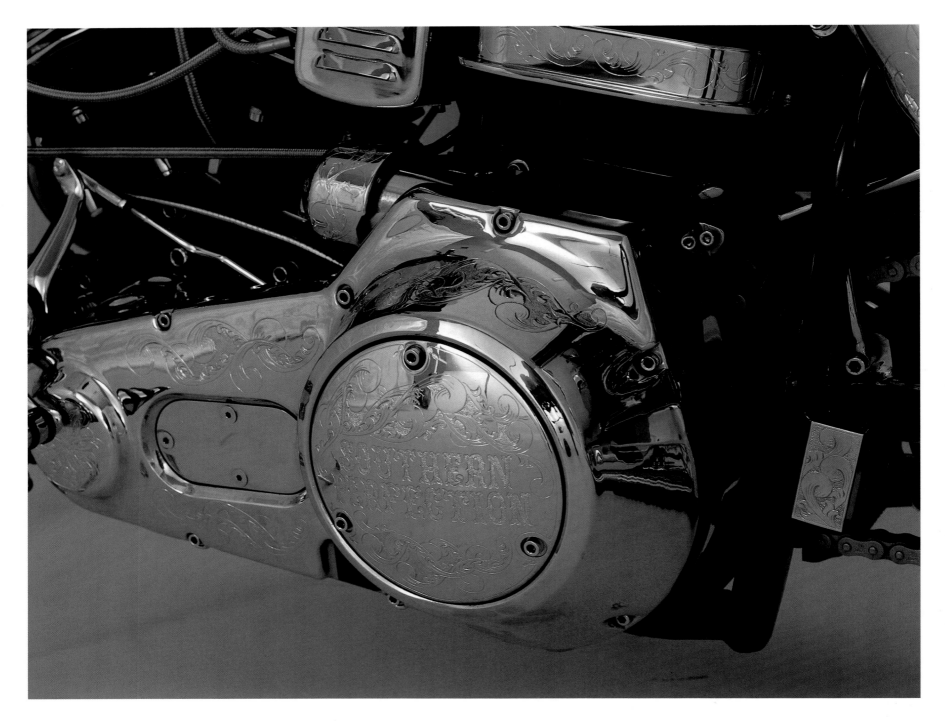

This attitude keeps custom bike shops like Arlen Ness, Dave Perewitz, Kennedy Custom Cycles, Bartels, the Parts Bin, and all the others busy year after year. But in this case, the owner himself was pretty handy with a wrench and had done most of the work himself. But there was the frame, that stock frame. Something custom was needed so he called up frame wizard Rick Doss who massaged and moulded a frame to order. Another name well known in the custom bike world is painter Teresa Crane who laid on the deep black cherry lacquer, Dan choosing a classic paint scheme with stylized flames. Note that the headlamp, usually chromed, is also painted to match.

This custom Shovel focuses on a more conservative look, maybe even subdued if such a word could ever describe a Harley Big Twin. While the engine was kept stock for reliability, it did find a few extra horsepower via an

An S&S two throat carburettor gives this engine extra hp.

S&S Twin Throat carburettor. It also breathes less restrictively thanks to a pair of Santee 2 in (51 mm) pipes which provide 'a more resonant exhaust note' (as in no mufflers).

Little details often make the difference between a first place winner and the rest of the competition. Items like the o-ring footpegs, the electrical cables sheathed in stainless steel braided lines, all add up to what is called the 'sanitary' look, very neat, very uncluttered so that the overall flow of the bike's aesthetics aren't interrupted. If it sounds like a work of art, it is. Even more to the point is the generous engraving gracing the cases and heads. Something you might see on a sterling silver tea service, but here the delicate swirls and curves contrast with and

bring out the massive nature of the 80 cu. in (1300cc) Harley powerplant.

Dan's daughter Paige often rides as a passenger on her father's custom show winner while Dan's wife rides her very own Milwaukee iron. It's nice for a family to share a common interest, especially an uncommonly outstanding Harley-Davidson.

Technical Specification

- Engine: 45° V-Twin, aircooled, stock bore and stroke, 3$\frac{7}{16}$ in (87 mm) × 3$\frac{31}{32}$ in (101 mm) displacement 80 cu. in (1300cc), approx. 60 bhp;
- Lubrication: dry sump, separate oil tank;
- Ignition: battery and coil, electric start and kick;
- Carburettor: S&S Twin Throat;
- Transmission: 4-speed H-D, footchange.

Hot Lime
"Wicked, Mean, Green and Nasty" FXSTC

Believe it or not, only a 10-year old boy had faith in this 1989 Heritage Softail Custom. It's builder, Paul de Meester, could not get any support from his adult friends when he came up with the idea to paint a Harley fluorescent green. Everybody told him, nobody paints Harleys green! Going against the prevailing status quo can get you in trouble or it can push you over the

Paul de Meester flaunted the prevailing design ethics by painting his Heritage Softail custom fluorescent green.

top. In this case the owner's creative convictions were the hot ticket to success. And it doesn't take a 10-year old kid to immediately know this custom is way cool, and way tasty . . . it's Hot Lime! And you won't see another bike quite like it even in a

hotbed of custom Harleys like Southern California.

It's owner, designer and builder, Paul de Meester got his introduction into the ultra-cool side of things at a very young age. Although born in Belgium, he grew up in Calgary, Canada and at 13 was earning his spending cash delivering newspapers on a little NSU

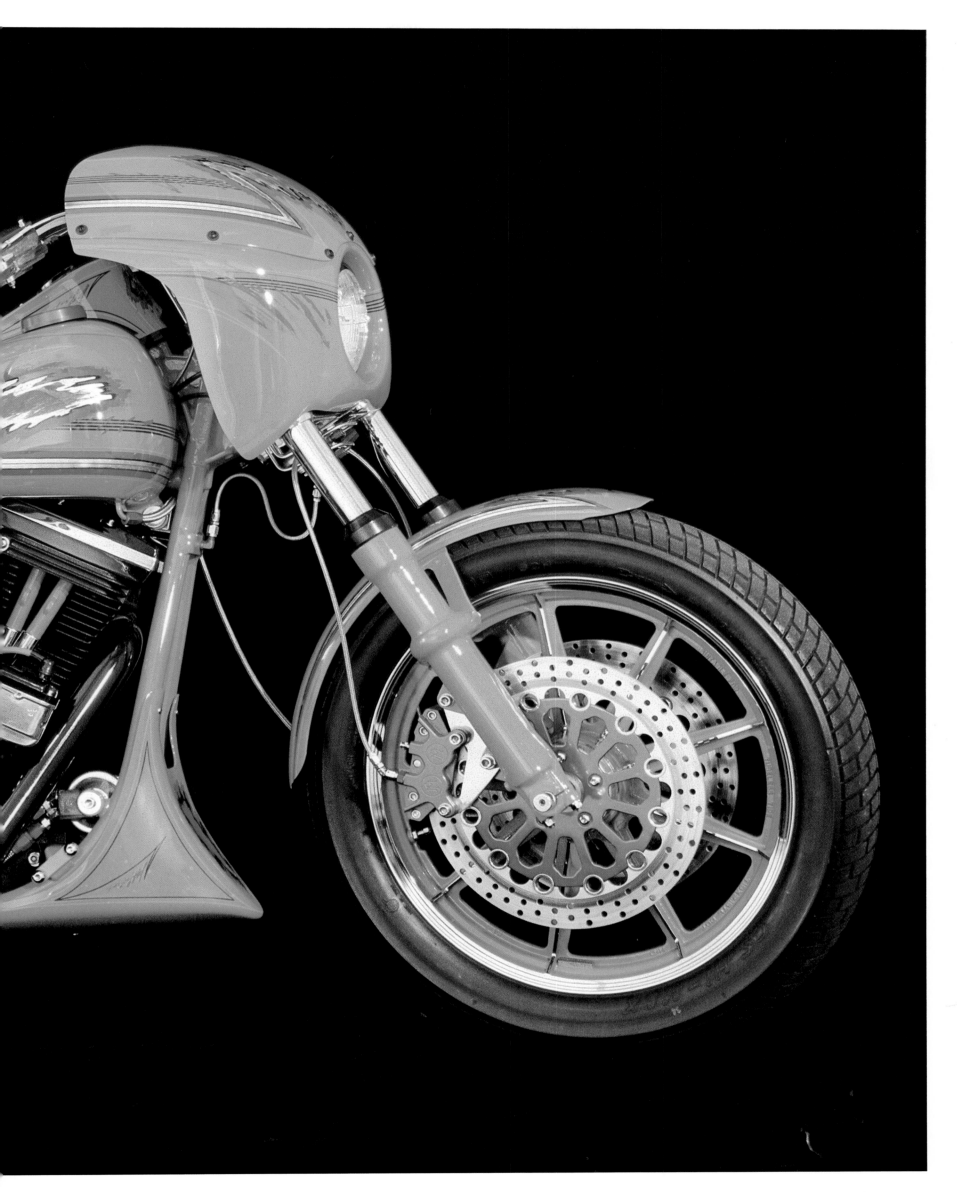

Prima scooter. Newspapers get delivered even in the middle of frigid Canadian winters and Paul easily remembers days at 40 degrees below zero . . . so cold that one morning, his bike's brakes froze!

Double 13 in (330 mm) disc brakes, both front and rear.

In the early '70s he moved to San Francisco and began making frames and gas and oil tanks for his own use and for a few friends. Paul's own

developing style was influenced by the famous custom Harley builder Arlen Ness. Arlen once painted Paul a very tricky paint job for one of his bikes . . . for the princely sum of $125! Of course that was 1972. The price of a custom

paint job has made a quantum leap and twenty years later, the cost of the Hot Lime's sizzling paint job reached the $5000 mark!

The inspiration for the radical paint

Other details include Arlen Ness handlebars.

job came from a visit to Palm Springs, CA during Spring Break, when thousands of college kids throw a big vacation party. Paul saw herds of cafe-

type non-Harley motorcycles all painted in fluorescent colours. Why not do a Harley up the same way? he asked his friends.

He got zero support from the adults,

only his buddy's 10-year old son, Ben, who was tapped into the latest trends, said go for it, that will be great . . . paint it Teen-age Mutant Ninja Turtle green!

Hot Lime was completed in six months with Paul as the main builder. Mechanically, the 80 cu. in (1300cc) Evo motor was kept stock except for a mild street Andrews cam and a 1.57 in (40 mm) Mikuni feeding fuel. It was also treated to the new Morris mag which features an automatic advance that on start-up runs retarded, then as soon as the engine fires, kicks to full advance, a sophisticated set-up just made for electric start needs.

A Wide Glide front end, shortened by 3 inches (76 mm), rolls an FXR 19 inch (483 mm) mag wheel which required custom spacers to fit into the WG forks. Performance Machine brakes were used fore and aft with the dual 13 in (330 mm) floaters requiring the skills of

Fred Muehlenhort at Race Tech (Oxnard, Ca) who made the addition of the right side brake possible. Fred also fabricated the 'hard-plumbing', as in rigid, stainless steel lines. Very tricky indeed.

Paul found the 2 in (51 mm) straight pipes at a swap meet, cut them down 6 inches (152 mm) shorter, then stripped, massaged, polished them, and lastly had them porcelain coated by Anderson Industry (Sante Fe Springs, Ca). The swingarm sports a one piece side mounted tail light made by Paul who also fabricated the seat. The special one piece licence bracket/brake caliper mount was cut from billet aluminium by Paul Berg at Turbo-Tech (Simi Valley, CA).

Paul removed the stock forward controls from the bike replacing them with '90 Sturgis brake, shifter and foot peg assemblies. The modification also makes room for the small front spoiler

from Rick Doss (Danville, VA) that sits below the Arlen Ness fairing.

The stock tank sports a Rick Doss dash, the inscription 'Wicked, Mean, Green and Nasty' and nearby the hot lime green tinted speedo is renumbered to 150 mph (241 km/h). Further refinements included Arlen Ness bars and grips with controls by PM. Highlighting the green are accents by Multi-Chrome (Oxnard, CA), powder coating by Bell Powder Coating (Ventura, CA) and shiny stuff by Coast Chrome and Polishing (Oxnard, CA).

Technical Specification

- Engine: 45° V-Twin, aircooled, 85 bhp, 80 cu. in (1300cc);
- Lubrication: dry sump, separate oil tank;
- Ignition: Morris magneto;
- Carburettor: 1.57 in (40 mm) Mikuni;
- Transmission: H-D 5 speed.

Another customised Softail.

XLH Sportster 883
'Special Custom'

Who says you cannot turn an 883 Sportster into a Big Twin? The builders at L.A. Harley-Davidson Middelharnis, Holland went to the limit on this one. First the Softail Custom was improved. All nuts, bolts, axles etc., were replaced with the stainless steel versions, and after having been thoroughly polished they cannot be distinguished from chrome. Thus the Sportster 883 was

L.A. Harley, Middelharnis transformed a standard 883 Sportster into a Big Twin.

transformed into a slightly smaller version of the Softail Custom.

So much work has been invested in this bike that it would be impossible to sum it up on one mere page. The Fat

Bob tank with enclosed dashboard panel was a must, even if it did mean a major redesign of most of the wiring. The medium Buckhorn handle bars offer a comfortable seating position, not too high, not too low, just right. To achieve a low sit on this standard frame they opted for a small 'solo-seat'.

The front end is in a Wide Glide style

with double brake calipers. The chromed headlight is a 4½ in (114 mm) mini-light. To ensure optimal grip, a 19 in (483 mm) spoked wheel was installed. By changing the length on the front fender struts the clearance was minimalised. The same result was achieved on the rear fender, keeping it low on the 16 in (406 mm) disc rear wheel, by mounting low shocks.

Seeing as they had to dismantle all the

A 1.57 in (40 mm) Screamin' Eagle carburettor was added to the Screamin' Eagle racing set.

engine covers to have them chromed anyway, a Screamin' Eagle race set with installed (just to finish it properly). Complemented by a 1.57 in (40 mm) Screamin' Eagle Carburettor this bike is raring to go!

Technical Specification

- Engine: 45° V-Twin Evolution, 55 cu. in (883cc);
- Horse Power: ample;
- Carburettor: 1.57 in (40 mm) Screamin' Eagle;
- Transmission: 4 speed; one-piece Fat Bob tank;
- Special paint: two-tone, red/cream G.L. Paints.

FXR Super Glide
'Big Boy'

Given the 25-odd new Harley models, you would think there would always be one to suit someone's wishes. However, nothing is farther from the truth. Reality shows that the real Harley enthusiast is never content with a 'standard' Harley. He will always feel a need to change at least something to personalise his bike. And that is exactly the opinion of the LA Harley David-

Sobriety is what makes this Harley so exceptional.

son people in Middelharnis, Holland. A Harley is not complete until you decide it is.

The FXR-Harley is greatly underrated

when it comes to almost unlimited custom possibilities. The Harley on these pages is a good example of the results one can achieve. A bike that achieves excellence and beauty through tasteful sobriety.

Technical details on this bike include: a Wide Glide front end with a Heritage conversion kit, a one piece Fat Bob

The classic '40–'50s look has become reality.

doesn't look much like a Sportster anymore.

A standard Sportster frame is too narrow to fit the large fender. The front of the fender was sawn off and a specially designed and developed polyester replacement was mounted to ensure the illusion of a prolonged fender.

The dash panel is a 1958 Hydra Glide model by CCI and the speedo features coloured numerals. Warning lights were mounted for: indicator lights, oil pressure, headlights and neutral. The wiring had to be extensively altered to fit all the new adaption.

The 16 in (406 mm) CCI chrome rear wheel sports R.V.S. spokes. A continental tyre complements the overall 'wide' impression initiated by the shorter-than-standard shocks with large chrome covers. The classical '40–'50s look is a reality.

Technical Specification

- Engine: 45° V-Twin Evolution 55 cu. in (883cc);
- Fenders front: flipskirted;
- Rear: hinged-Heritage;
- Solo-country saddle;
- 1¾ in (44 mm) drag pipes with Fishtail muffler;
- Springer headlight;
- Beehive tail light;
- Forward controls;
- Classic Super handle bars;
- Two-tone (black/cream) GL Paints.